THE LITTLE BOOK OF
CALM

PAUL WILSON

A PLUME BOOK

PLUME
Published by the Penguin Group
Penguin Putnam Inc., 375 Hudson Street, New York, New York 10014, U.S.A.
Penguin Books Ltd, 27 Wrights Lane, London W8 5TZ, England
Penguin Books Australia Ltd, Ringwood, Victoria, Australia
Penguin Books Canada Ltd, 10 Alcorn Avenue, Toronto, Ontario, Canada M4V 3B2
Penguin Books (N.Z.) Ltd, 182–190 Wairau Road, Auckland 10, New Zealand

Penguin Books Ltd, Registered Offices: Harmondsworth, Middlesex, England

Published by Plume, a member of Penguin Putnam Inc.
First published in Australia by Penguin Books Australia Ltd.

First American Printing, January, 1997
10 9 8 7 6 5

Ⓟ REGISTERED TRADEMARK—MARCA REGISTRADA

ISBN 0-452-27793-0

Printed in the United States of America

I've written this little book to be an on-hand comfort to you. Carry it with you to steal moments of peace and tranquillity. At any time, in any place.

Follow its recommendations and you will remain calm. Even in the most difficult moments.

And, most useful of all, when you feel troubled simply let this book fall open — let your intuition guide you — and you will see the most effective way for you to find calm at that particular moment.

Trust your intuition and you will become calm.

CARRY A PIECE
OF THE QUIET

Concentrate on silence.
When it comes, dwell on what
it sounds like.

Then strive to carry
that quiet with you
wherever you go.

WASTE SOME TIME

Hard-working people never waste
time on frivolous, fun-filled activities.
Yet, for hard-working people,
any time spent this way is
far from wasted.

SELECT YOUR COMPANY WELL

As harsh as it may sound, mixing with highly stressed people will make you feel stressed.

On the other hand, mixing with calm people – even for the briefest period -- will leave you feeling calm.

Be captivated
by your breath

When you dwell on the sound of
your breathing, when you can really
hear it coming and going, peace will
not be far behind.

PAUSE BETWEEN CHANGES

There's always a temptation to lump
all your life changes into one big
masochistic event.

Do your stress levels a favour and
take on changes one at a time.

INVEST IN A FRUIT BOWL

The more beautiful your fruit bowl,
the better stocked it is, the less
likely you are to turn to
stress-enhancing snack foods.

Eat more fruit, and you'll feel more
relaxed – it's as sweet as that.

DISREGARD SMALL ISSUES

The most important skill in
staying calm is not to lose sleep
over small issues. The second most
important skill is to be able to view
all issues as small issues.

START TEN MINUTES
EARLY

Start every journey ten minutes early.
Not only will you avoid the stress
of haste, but if all goes well
you'll have ten minutes to relax
before your next engagement.

WORRY WHEN
THE TIME COMES

Most worries are future-based.
They revolve around things that,
in most cases, will *never* happen.

Concentrate on the present and
the future will take care of itself.

SIP A PEPPERMINT

If you substitute a herbal tea such as peppermint for more stimulating drinks such as coffee and tea, your ability to be calm will be enhanced many times.

ADMIT YOU FEEL CALM

If you want to trick your subconscious into helping you feel calm, simply repeat: 'Every moment I feel calmer and calmer.'

WEAR SENSIBLE SHOES

Any reflexologist will tell you that
true relaxation begins at the feet.
It seems obvious, but wearing
comfortable shoes is nearly as
relaxing as wearing no shoes at all.

SEEK THE BEST IN EVERYTHING

Make a practice of looking for the best in people and situations. You'll find that simple approach induces optimism and positivity — both of which lead to calm.

BRUSH OR BE BRUSHED

Take the time to brush someone's
hair. Better still, brush your own –
or have someone else do it. Slowly,
methodically, extensively. (It
massages several calming acupressure
points,
and the repetition works wonders.)

PRETEND YOU'RE HUMAN

Leave it to others to be perfect,
to be wonderful. Be content with
what you are – you'll be much more
relaxed as a result.

START CHRISTMAS NOW

It probably took a lot of trial and
error over the centuries, but
Christmas carols and lullabies have a
unique ability to soothe.

Use them (silently) all year round.

SINGLE OUT SIMPLE PLEASURES

Approach something with your full attention and an open mind, and you'll find pleasure and complexity in it. A bunch of grapes. Or a glass of water. Or a field of grass. Or a sky of clouds.

All of such things can lead to calm.

JETTISON THE PAST

There is seldom any rational reason
for having regrets about past deeds or
events. Because the past does not
exist in any way other than in
your memory.

When you recognise this lack of
reality, you can be calm.

TAKE JUNIOR LESSONS

Take a lesson in calmness from
children: watch how they live
every moment for the pleasure
of the moment.

Pretend, and you could be
like that, too.

THINK CALM

Have calm thoughts.
Picture calm scenes.
Recall calm sounds.

And guess what you'll be feeling . . .

STEAL THIRTY SECONDS

When you're tense, go somewhere
quiet – even the bathroom will do at a
pinch – and take thirty seconds to
gather your thoughts, and work out
how you're going to become calm.

They could be the most useful
thirty seconds in your day.

CLEAR OUT THE CLUTTER

Physical disarray adds
to the tension of life.
Clearing out the clutter
is an orderly way to calm.

STIMULATE WITH INTENT

Recognise that there is a time for
stimulation and a time for calm. This
means never trying to fool yourself
that a stimulant can help you to relax.

SPRAY ORANGE BLOSSOM

Add three drops of orange blossom oil
(neroli) to a cup of mineral water,
and spray it from an atomiser when
you need to feel relaxed.

IGNORE SMALL PRINT

Small print is custom-designed to induce frustration. If you want to stay calm, have someone else read (and explain) the small type for you.

PAT SOMETHING

Share your life with a pet — being
generous with your affection to it —
and you'll have an appreciative
assistant in your efforts to
become calm.

FORGIVE ON THE SPOT

To bear ill-feelings towards someone else is more damaging to the bearer than the recipient.

For your own sake, forgive quickly and freely.

BARRICADE THE DOOR

There comes a time when you need to
shut yourself off from interruption, to
concentrate on your own needs
and responsibilities.

Do it for at least one hour a day.

LEVITATE

Stand straighter and taller than you
believe feels natural, with an *imaginary*
thread attached to the top of your
skull lifting you a few millimetres
above the ground.

The higher above the ground you feel,
the closer you will be to feeling calm.

TOUCH OR BE TOUCHED

The human touch is one of the surest
ways of unburdening stresses. Just as
the embrace of a parent soothes the
upset child, just as a kiss or
handshake takes the sting out of an
argument, the simplest touch
sometimes works miracles.

PAINT THE TOWN GREEN

Plants pour oxygen into the environment while soaking up carbon dioxide and pollutants. Keep plants where you work, sleep and live, and you'll enjoy more oxygen.

The more oxygen you can get, the calmer you will become.

LOOK FOR THE PLEASURE IN CALM

Unlike muscle building, techniques for
creating calm work better when there
is no pain, no effort.

In fact, being calm is in itself
one of life's great pleasures.

UNWIND WITH
AN APHRODISIAC

Ginseng, which has been coveted for
its aphrodisiac properties for
centuries, also has a reputation for
being able to relax the nervous system
if taken regularly.

LOWER THE CROSSBAR

One of the greatest strains in life is constantly having to live up to the standards we set for ourselves.

Do yourself a favour and – from time to time – relax those standards a little.

LEARN TWO TAI CHI EXERCISES

It is almost impossible to feel tense
when you're concentrating on
a Tai Chi routine.

Learn the basic Tai Chi exercises and
you have a secret to becoming calm.

LISTEN FOR THE QUIET

Quiet is the essence of calm. You cannot *force* quiet, you can only accept it when it comes. But if you listen for it, really listen, you will find it in the most unexpected places.

All it takes is a little concentration.

REST YOUR FINGERS

Gently rest the thumb and fingertips
of one hand against the corresponding
thumb and fingertips of the other. Just
the lightest touch. Breathe slowly for
sixty seconds and allow the calm
to overtake you.

WEAR WHITE

The clothes you wear have a distinct influence on the way you feel. Loose garments, natural fabrics and light colours all lead to calm.

This is why yogis wear white.

SELL YOUR WRISTWATCH

Have you ever noticed how relaxed
you feel the moment you remove your
watch? Remove yours from time to
time, and remove yourself from time
pressures.

BE NEGATIVE ABOUT IONS

Negative ions are remarkable things.
They freshen the air, assist your
breathing, enhance your mood and
induce feelings of calm and energy.

All it takes is a low-cost negative ion
generator (ioniser). Or an
electrical storm.

RUB ON A ROSE

Massage is one of the most
pleasurable ways to be soothed into a
state of relaxation. By adding a little
rose oil to your massage oil you can
make the experience doubly effective.

MAKE FOR THE
STRAIGHT BACK

Oddly enough, the chairs that help
you relax most may not be the lazy,
over-stuffed variety that immediately
springs to mind. A chair that supports
your back, and helps you to sit erect,
is probably your best choice.

DECLARE TODAY
A HOLIDAY

Imagine every day is a holiday. Do
one little thing that stimulates this
holiday mood each day, then watch
your worries fade away.

PLAY A CALM ROLE

Pretend you are calm: adopt the
characteristics of a calm person,
pretend that others see you as a calm
person, and in no time you'll be a
calm person.

RUN FOR YOUR LIFE

Running is one of life's antidotes to
stress. It's simple, requires no special
training and it begins to take effect
within the first 200 metres.

REFLECT ON BEAUTY

Do this, not for the stimulation, but for the elevation. Because you'll find calm where you find beauty – regardless of whether it is natural or man-made.

SLEEP LIKE A BABY

Anything that interferes with your
sleep – coffee, cola, alcohol – interferes
with your ability to become calm.

Do whatever is necessary to get as
much sleep as you feel you need.

STRIDE FOR
SHEER DELIGHT

While some forms of exercise may
seem torturous, walking is easy and
pleasurable. Walk every day – not
because you have to, but because if
you combine it with the right attitude,
it can be the most relaxing way to get
from A to B.

SNATCH A COUPLE
OF MINUTES

If you feel you need it, take brief cat
naps throughout the day. You'll be
surprised at how much peace can come
from a couple of minutes – even while
sitting at your typewritezzzzzzzz
zzzzzzzzzzzzzzzzzzzzzzzzzz
zzzzzzzzzzzzz
zzzzzzz

START IN THE RAW

Start every meal with something raw —
fruit or vegetables. Not only do these
'alkaline foods' enhance feeling of
calm, they add harmony to a meal.

PAMPER YOUR FEET

Soak your feet, then massage them
with moisturiser or a relaxing
combination of essential oils.

You'll be blissfully relaxed in no
time.

TAKE THE BACK SEAT

However much you think you might
enjoy driving, it is a stressful
business. Take the back seat (with a
driver you trust), and spend the
journey sharing your calm.

CONTROL ONLY WHAT
YOU CAN CONTROL

Be rigorous in differentiating between
what is achievable and what is a
waste of time. Then devote your
energies only to those tasks you can
achieve (pass on the others to
someone else).

SIMPLIFY

The fewer things you must do in life,
the fewer things you own, manage or
are responsible for, the fewer are the
stresses that accompany them.

RESORT TO POLITENESS

Practise politeness, not for the benefit
of others, but for the ennoblement of
yourself. It doesn't matter if the
receivers reciprocate (which they
usually will) or not – you will feel
better for your niceness.

RECOGNISE THE

DIFFERENCE

BETWEEN HAVING

AND LIVING

THINK WARM

A cold body is seldom calm. Rubbing
the hands together, furiously,
helps you to feel warm.

Feeling calm follows feeling warm.

DEVELOP A TASTE
FOR FISH

Why are fish so relaxing to watch?
Because they move slowly and,
perhaps more importantly, because
they breathe slowly.

Merely watching them is like
gazing on a seascape.

PICTURE YOURSELF

Picture yourself on an idyllic South
Pacific island. See yourself on the
sun-bleached sands. Note what you're
wearing, the relaxed way you're
standing, the way the breeze blows
your hair, the calm, semi-smile on
your face.

Now imagine what it *feels* like
to be there.

TAKE A LONG CUT

There's nothing like a change to break the stress patterns that build throughout the day. Every now and then make a point of doing something you wouldn't normally do – like taking a different route home from work.

Use the time to appreciate the change.

PLAN YOUR WORRIES

Put aside a certain amount of time
each day – at the same time each day –
which you devote to sorting through
your worries.

When the time is up, stop worrying.

MASSAGE YOUR TEMPLES

Some of the most powerful calming acupressure points can be found at the temples. Apply a light pressure as you breathe out, ease the pressure as you breathe in.

BE POSITIVE ABOUT BEING POSITIVE

Work on having positive thoughts,
pay particular attention to speaking
positive words, then let the resultant
positive feelings take care of
everything else.

TURTLE

The pace you move has a direct
relationship with the way you feel.
Slow down your movements,
consciously relax your gestures and
expressions, and before you know it
you'll be relaxed.

DISCOVER

It's hard to feel tense when you're learning something you want to know.

And you can learn from the most unlikely places.

FINGER THE BEADS

Use up the nervous energy that
concentrates in the fingers and hands
by fingering worry beads.

MAKE LOVE

The relaxation that follows
love-making works on
many different levels.

IGNORE THE PHONE ONCE

You only have to leave a phone
ringing once or twice in your life to
appreciate that important calls
always ring back.

One less pressure in your life.

GO LIMP

Really tense one set of muscles – such as the arms or legs – then quickly let them go limp. The contrast between 'tense' and 'relaxed' should indicate what 'relaxed' really feels like.

Dwell on that feeling.

FIND WONDER
IN ALL YOU DO

There is little doubt that those who
get the most from life are those who
look for the wonder in even the
smallest things they do. Cultivate this
skill and you'll find peace and
satisfaction as well.

RECOGNISE ADDICTION

Satisfying cravings of any kind
(nicotine, chocolate, caffeine, alcohol)
is no way to help yourself feel calm.
Recognise addictions for what they
are, and find an alternative.

Then you can be calm.

SIP WARM WATER

A glass of chilled water will calm you
more than most other liquids.

A cup of *warm* water will calm you
even more.

TAKE A
LONG DISTANCE VIEW

Your eyes are at their most relaxed
when they focus on distant scenes —
especially natural ones.

And when your eyes are relaxed, your
body starts to relax.

FACE A WET TOWEL

As any beauty therapist or barber will
tell you, nothing soaks away facial
stress and tension quite so efficiently
as a damp, hot towel.

GO ON, SMILE

A smile relaxes all the major facial
muscles. It also sets off an emotional
chain reaction that invariably helps
you feel good.

ACCEPT ONLY
ONE DEADLINE

Deadlines are at the root of so many
stress problems. Take on only one
deadline at a time, and you will
become master of your own time.

FLOAT

Float in a swimming pool, a float tank,
or even a bathtub, and weightlessly
feel your tensions dissolve.

MAKE MAGNANIMITY
A HABIT

Indulge yourself by being generous —
help someone out, perform an act of
kindness, offer a compliment.

The person who will feel most uplifted
by you having done so is ... you.

GO FROM A TO B

While vitamin A foods enhance your
ability to feel calm, it is the vitamin B
foods that are known to have the most
dynamic effect. Include beans, lentils,
peas, nuts, seeds, wheatgerm,
wholegrains, dairy foods in your diet.

KNOW WHEN
TO WITHDRAW

There comes a time in every struggle
when determination serves no purpose
and becomes an end unto itself.

Knowing when to move on to the next
issue is a skill possessed by many
calm people.

REAFFIRM YOUR FRIENDSHIPS

If you tend to get overly serious
about your work or your
responsibilities, remind yourself that
the most common deathbed regrets
relate to neglected relationships, not
unfinished business.

TURN OFF THE LIGHTS

When all else fails in a stressful day,
go somewhere quiet and dark, and
listen to your breathing as you ease
into a state of relaxation.

DICTATE THE PACE

Just as a group attitude or mood can
influence the individual, a determined
individual can influence the group.
By moving slowly, speaking calmly,
you can spread a feeling of calm
within a group.

PRACTISE SAYING NO

There is only so much you can achieve before affecting your efficiency and state of mind.

Only take on what you can do – then politely, but firmly, turn down all other requests.

WRITE DOWN YOUR WORRY

It's marvellous how quickly many worries dissolve when you write them down on a piece of paper – then review the likelihood of them eventuating.

Nine times out of ten that likelihood will be remote.

PUT YOUR FEET UP

There's more to the simple act of
putting your feet up than
improved circulation.

It quickly leads to feelings
of relaxation.

STOCKPILE BEAUTIFUL MOMENTS

Write them down, keep a photo, keep
a record in your computer. Then
recall these moments often, reflecting
on them, taking pleasure in them,
integrating them into your day-to-day
routine and outlook.

GROW YOUR OWN

Gardeners are among the most calm
and relaxed people (while they're
gardening) you'll find.

SET YOUR OWN AGENDA

If you set your own agenda, and don't
allow others to dictate your pace too
much, you will have much more time
to become calm.

CARESS THE BACK
OF YOUR HAND

In Zone Therapy, the backs of the
hands are the way to tap into calm.
The lightest possible upwards stroke
with the fingertips helps to induce
a relaxed state.

PRUNE PRESSURE
PHRASES

Pressure phrases like 'I have to', 'I must', 'I should', 'I don't have the time', exacerbate feelings of stress. Listen for such words in your thoughts and speech, then replace them with more relaxed phrases – 'I may', 'I choose to', 'I will make the time'.

HAVE LITTLE SUCCESSES

There's nothing like a degree of
success to help you become relaxed.
Even if it's only with the most trivial
activities, make room for yourself to
succeed from time to time.

WATCH OUT FOR
TENSE PEOPLE

Learn to recognise signs of tension
and anxiety in others. In this way you
can be aware of your own physiology,
and can work towards becoming calm.

APPRECIATE THE ROUTINE

Any task you can do on remote
control has potential as a way of
helping you to feel good. Treat it as a
meditation, concentrating wholly on
the moment, and you will be fulfilled.

BREATHE LESS

A deeply relaxed person breathes only
5–8 times a minute. By slowing your
breathing down to that rate, you will
quickly relax.

ADD A DAB OF LAVENDER

A dab of lavender not only eases
aches and pains, but works wonders
in helping you to relax.

REDISCOVER MILK

Mother was right! Milk helps you to relax and become calm. (It is rich in calcium, a muscle relaxant, as well as an amino acid called tryptophan, a powerful natural sedative.)

PRETEND YOU BELIEVE

Regardless of what you know, by
pretending to be absolutely calm and
relaxed, you will fool your
subconscious into believing you are
calm and relaxed.

WEAR DONALD DUCK
UNDERPANTS

Choose a few childlike accoutrements
to remind you of the irreverent,
uninhibited, joyous side of life.

MAKE YOUR
WORK IMPORTANT

The difference between abject
drudgery and noble, uplifting work is
often no more than perspective.

Treat your work as important, and the
satisfaction that flows will work
towards helping you unwind.

BICKER ON SCHEDULE

While it's impossible to avoid all
conflict and arguments, it *is* possible
not to feel too bad when they happen.
Simply postpone the argument.

Agree to discuss the issues in detail,
at some later date ... and be surprised
at how peacefully that can happen.

SHAMPOO SANS SHAMPOO

You access the calming acupressure
points at the top of the head in the
most pleasurable way through scalp
massage – the actions of a shampoo,
but without the shampoo.

GAZE ON SOMETHING BLUE

Or pink. Sometimes green.
Each of these colours – one warm, two
cool – has the magical ability to instil
calm in a troubled mind.

REST IN A TUB

A leisurely, warm bath soothes like
no other method. Lower the lights,
add a few drops of your favourite oil,
and you'll be transported.

LOVE THE MOMENT

When you concentrate your attention
on absorbing every detail of every
moment — savouring every taste,
hearing every sound, noting every
colour — you will be calm
before you know it.

TRAIN A CALM PLACE

If you practise being calm in a certain place – say, a favourite chair or park bench – soon your subconscious will associate feelings of calm with that particular place.

Then simply go there to become calm.

KNOW WHEN TO STOP

For most activities in life, there are
no prizes for perseverance. When you
know your stress levels are rising,
stop what you're doing – either take a
break or do something else.

SPREAD BEAUTY

Wherever you go in life, whatever
you do, make a conscious effort to add
a little beauty, or to contribute to the
beauty that's already there.

OFFER A COMPLIMENT

You'll find the good feelings that flow
from it will be as much yours as
the recipient's.

TAKE ALL THE TIME
IN THE WORLD

Contrary to what you may tell yourself, you have all the time in the world to do whatever you choose.

What cannot be fitted into your day, cannot be done – forget about it

DELEGATE RUTHLESSLY

The more you delegate, the more
comfortable and capable you become
with the practice.

Then, the more you delegate, the less
pressure you have to live with.

THANK YOUR
GOOD HUMOUR

Get on speaking terms with your
humour. Play games with it. Access it
more than you think is a good
thing ... and it will help you to
become calm.

MASSAGE YOUR EYEBROWS

You do this intuitively when under
pressure – now you can do it
consciously. Work the relaxing
acupressure points around the
forehead by massaging your eyebrows
in an outwards direction.

LEARN TO LOVE CHANGE

If you appreciate that as much good
comes from change as bad, you will
avoid the concerns that many people
seem to have about it.

Relax and be open to change
when it visits.

SLEEP ON A PATCHOULI PILLOW

Add three drops of patchouli or chamomile oils to your pillow every few nights for a blissfully calm sleep.

SHED A FEW TEARS

There is something both emotionally
and physically soothing about crying.

VISUALISE A SUNSET

Even though sunsets may sometimes be
sad, they are always peaceful.

And pink ones are even more
peaceful.

BREAK THE PATTERN

When you find yourself under
pressure, do something different.
Stand where you wouldn't normally
stand, sit where you wouldn't
normally sit, think the way you
wouldn't normally think.

SAY YOUR PRAYERS

If you have spiritual or religious
beliefs, you probably have access to
one of the world's most time-
honoured methods of achieving
tranquillity: prayer.

PRETEND

IT'S SATURDAY

SWITCH OFF OR
SWITCH ON

Electric lights, television, computers,
fluorescent lights ... all add to
feelings of tension.

Ironically, you can compensate for
them with another electronic
implement – an ioniser.

BE UP FOR THE SUNRISE

It is no coincidence that serious
meditators, yogis, ascetics, martial
artists, and many religious orders
treat the moments before sunrise as
the most precious of the day.

TAKE TO THE WAVES

Sea air, salt water and the sound of
waves – all contribute to a growing
sense of calm.

GET IT OFF YOUR CHEST

Articulating your problems often takes
you half the way to solving them.
Share your feelings and problems with
someone else and you will feel more
peaceful.

MAKE FRIENDS
WITH A MASSEUR

Or a beauty therapist.

BE CONSCIOUS
OF CHOICES

Whether you recognise them or not,
you usually have choices. The art is
to recognise them.

Because when you can see your
choices, you will feel free.

THINK BEFORE YOU BUY

To avoid the stresses of debt, think
about what you can afford to spend,
long before you think about what
you'd like to buy.

Sweat

Physical exertion counters the
negative effects of stress and helps
you to feel good about yourself.

Exercise until there is a light film of
sweat on your brow, then continue for
twenty more minutes.

HOLD THE WORDS BACK

When you're under pressure, words
come quickly and the rhythm of your
speech speeds up. By reversing these
patterns – slowing your words,
articulating your thoughts more
carefully, slowing your breathing –
you can beguile your subconscious
into believing you are relaxed.

CALM DOWN YOUR DIET

If you want to feel calm, eat more
raw fruit and vegetables, yoghurt,
milk, eggs, wholegrains, beans, pulses,
nuts and seeds.

WATCH YOUR HEAD

Most stress and anxiety is the result
of what happens inside your head,
rather than what happens to
your body.

Take comfort in the fact that most
things which take place in your
thoughts *never* eventuate.

LEAVE TOWN

It is more relaxing to walk down a country road than a suburban street. It is more comforting to gaze on rolling hills than on rolling stock.

It is more relaxing to sail in the wide open sea than it is on a busy harbour.

SMELL THE BLOOMS

Certain scents stimulate the
production of the relaxing chemical,
serotonin, in the brain.

Among the more effective of these
scents are lavender and chamomile.

APPRECIATE LIFE IN
3/4 TIME

Not only is the waltz one of the most
lighthearted and joyous of musical
forms, it can also be the
most soothing.

Think 3/4 time as you walk, and feel
the joy in your step.

SIT IN A CHURCH

Regardless of what you believe in,
churches and temples are
extraordinary places of peace.

Take a pew and absorb the atmosphere
of absolute peace and calm that
permeates them.

PRESS ON THE ROOF

Tense people have tense jaw muscles.
To relieve this tension, simply press
on the roof of the mouth, behind the
front teeth, with your tongue.

TURN INTO A WINDMILL

Imagine a windmill turning. Copy
those actions with your arms,
transcribing a great slow-motion arc –
and you will wave yourself calm.

FROWN DARKLY

Tighten your forehead and eyebrows into a tight, ugly frown. Then raise your eyebrows and feel the tension lift.

Remember the feeling of relaxation that follows.

DANCE TILL YOU DROP

One of the most pleasurable exercises
around, uninhibited dancing distracts
even the most committed worrier.

COVER YOUR FACE

Place the palm of a hand on each side
of your face – from your lips to your
eyes, allowing room for your nose –
and apply a light pressure until you
feel relaxed.

SHELVE YOUR WORRIES

Decide on a way of storing your
worries each evening before you go to
bed. Whisper them into an envelope
or write them in a diary, then store
and forget them.

Chances are they'll be greatly
reduced, if not solved, by morning.

EAT 80:20

The ideal calm diet maintains a ratio
of alkalines (wholegrains, cereals,
vegetables, etc.) to acids (coffee,
meat, sugar, processed foods,
preservatives, etc.) of about 80:20.

BACH TO THE RESCUE

The most well-known Bach treatment,
Rescue Remedy, produces a calming
effect in trying situations as diverse
as major traumas through to
little anxieties.

ANYTHING FOR A LAUGH

Remain on the lookout for things that
make you laugh – and, if you see
nothing worth laughing at,
pretend you see it.

Then laugh.

WRITE IT DOWN

Write down your concerns and be
surprised at how quickly they dissolve
when you read them on paper.

MAKE AN APPOINTMENT

Make an appointment with yourself to
deal with worries at a specific time
in the future.

The more seriously you treat that
appointment, the more efficiently
you'll deal with the problem.

EMPLOY YOUR
SUBCONSCIOUS

Your subconscious specialises in
finding solutions to your most
personal problems.

Place your faith in it, and give your
conscious mind a rest.

MEDITATE

Concentrate on a movement, a sound,
an image, a thought — without strain
and without concern if your attention
wanders.

Before you know it, you will be
meditating.

AVOID COGS
TWICE A DAY

Twice a day, spend a few minutes not
being a cog in the machine – take a
walk around the block, have a nap
under the desk, deliver the mail to the
post office, abandon your routine – it
will add variety and vitality
to your day.

GIVE YOURSELF
PERMISSION

Find a quiet place, regularly, and say
out loud: 'For five minutes in every
hour, I give myself permission to
relax and to be calm.'

Keep repeating it to yourself.

ONLY WORRY ABOUT
BIG THINGS

If you can overlook the small issues
of life, and concentrate on the
important ones, you will be much
closer to calm.

ALIGHT ONE STOP EARLY

If you consciously set out to break
your own routines, you can also break
your worry habits. Take a different
road home, get off the bus a stop
early, talk to a stranger, and absorb
the differences.

CHANGE

There are only two ways to handle
tense situations: you can change them,
or you can change the way
you look at them.

There is enlightenment to be had in
changing the way you look at things.

USE A SOFT VOICE

Have you ever noticed a calm person
with a loud voice?

BE NICE

As unfashionable as the sentiment may
seem, nice people find fewer
impediments to becoming calm.

ABOUT THE AUTHOR

Paul Wilson is the author of *Instant Calm*,
The Calm Technique and *Calm at Work*. Known as
"the King of Calm," he is one of the world's leading
authorities on relaxation. The chairman of a Sydney
advertising agency, he also works as a communications
consultant and serves as director of a hospital.
He is a noted public speaker and the
author of two novels. He lives in Australia.